LAMENT FOR A NATION: THEN AND NOW

RON DART

AMERICAN ANGLICAN PRESS
New York

American Anglican Press, Empire Building, 71 Broadway, Level 2B – No 149, New York, New York 10006.

Front cover image by Barbara Christian.

ISBN: 978-0-9963248-0-9

Printed in the United States of America.

PREFACE

2015 signals the 50th anniversary of the publication of George Grant's prophetic missive, *Lament for a Nation: The Defeat of Canadian Nationalism*. Much has happened in the USA and Canada between 1965 and 2015. The much older and time tried High Toryism, that Grant so defended in *Lament,* has become an endangered species as the tribalism of the left and right, liberal and conservative ideologies wage their ongoing battles to define the future of North American culture and politics.

It is significant to note that when *Lament for a Nation* was published in 1965 another missive of equal import was published a couple of years later—these two political tracts for the times, when read side by side, make it abundantly clear the differences between a more classical High Tory political vision and the more philistine-like and populist turn to conservatism. *Political Realignment: A Challenge to Thoughtful Canadians* was published in 1967 (Confederation year for Canada). The book was written by the Honorable Ernest Manning (Premier of Alberta) and Ernest Manning's son, Preston Manning, did much of the research for the "challenge to thoughtful Canadians". Both books claim to embody a conservative response to liberalism and the Liberal Party in Canada, but Grant's *Lament* and Manning's *Political Realignment* track in different directions. Most of the principles that Manning holds high are bourgeois liberal, whereas Grant was convinced such a notion of conservatism negated an older and deeper notion of what is worth conserving. The Manning dynasty (father and son) in Alberta and *Political Realignment* have very much won the day in Canadian political life with the negation of the Progressive Conservative Party and the rise of Harperism. There is a direct line and lineage, in short, from the principles and ideas articulated in *Political Realignment* and the form of conservatism that dominates Canada and much of republicanism in the United States.

Lament for a Nation is drawn from the classical Biblical notion of *Lamentations* that can be found in the Hebrew canon—Grant was, in short, a modern Jeremiah who saw all too clearly what was afoot in culture, philosophy, theology, education and politics. Grant, like Jeremiah, also saw the implications and consequences of questionable decisions—he probed the crude, benign and sophisticated forms of liberalism, enucleated what liberalism enfolded us within and revealed what such enfolding looked like when unfolded. Grant held high for all to see the inner sanctum and nature of liberalism in which freedom, power, calculative reason, individualism, choice, equality and willing were the unquestioned and unquestionable dogma and creed of the modern and, soon to be, postmodern ethos and world.

Lament for a Nation is not only a lament for Canada at a symptomatic political party level—it is much more about a lament for the passing away of a way of seeking for and living from the "Good"— Grant's turn to the Platonic "Good" with its older and wiser way of understanding contemplative theology, philosophy and politics comes as a corrective and antidote to the Western addiction to the *vita activa* that so dominates the driven and relentless West. The turn that Grant pointed to was a turn to the deeper *vita contemplativa* that was at the heart and core of Classical and Christian theological, philosophical and political thought and life. *Lament for a Nation* is a lament, therefore, about the way a driven and ambitious form of liberalism has banished the contemplative way and enthroned the active way (with many a reward for those who genuflect to such a reigning monarch). The final chapter in *Lament* ponders whether the seeming "necessity" of the liberal *vita activa* is a needful imperative and a good—such a prophetic way of thinking is certainly not found in *Political Realignment* (and the clan that bow before and are disciples of such a missive).

Lament for a Nation: Then and Now includes four essays: two of the articles deal directly with *Lament* and Red Toryism—one article touches on Sheila Grant's "Afterword" that was included in a later edition of *Lament.* I have also included an essay on George Grant and Allen Ginsberg. Both men, in their different ways, wrote missives that challenged the hegemony of liberalism and its unfolding: Ginsberg's *Howl* and Grant's *Lament,* at one level, seem to have much in common— but, do they? The High Toryism of Grant and political anarchism of Ginsberg, when day is done, do move in different directions—both men do agree there is much to howl against and lament, but they definitely differ on what is the best, finest and fittest way forward—they do agree on what they want to be free from—they are not on the same page or path to be taken on what they want to be free for.

My hope is that this little book will highlight the perennial significance of *Lament* both when it was published in 1965 and for 2015 and beyond—there is indeed, much to ponder 50 years after the publication of *Lament for a Nation* and what was seen and signalled in this jeremiad.

Ron Dart, Eastertide 2015

GEORGE GRANT:
LAMENT FOR A NATION AND RED TORYISM

Introduction

Lament for a Nation is a classic missive within the genre of Canadian political philosophy—when the book was published in 1965, Grant ignited the nationalist New Left in Canada, challenged and questioned the notion that conservatism is necessarily right of centre and exposed the vulnerable core of liberalism. ***Lament for a Nation*** emerged from the 1963 Federal election in which Tommy Douglas (NDP) supported Lester Pearson (Liberal) to bring down the minority Conservative government of Prime Minister John Diefenbaker. President J.F. Kennedy backed Pearson's bid for power contra Diefenbaker in 1963 and Grant saw in this liberal alliance of Kennedy-Pearson the death knell of a deeper and older conservatism that had played a significant role in the shaping of the Canadian ethos. It was the passing away of such a "Tory touch" that Grant lamented, jeremiad like, that is at the core of ***Lament for a Nation***. Grant moves in a deft and firm footed way, chapter by chapter, in ***Lament*** from the actual historic election, to an analysis of Diefenbaker (the good and bad) to the history and differences between liberalism and classical conservatism to political philosophy, philosophy and theology. The book embodies a distinctive and unique way of doing political philosophy and the conclusions Grant reached earned him the honorific title (given by Gad Horowitz but never fully embraced by Grant) of "Red Tory".

This essay will discuss the historic background to ***Lament for a Nation***, the way Grant does political philosophy in ***Lament***, the content of ***Lament*** and Grant's ambiguous attitude towards the language of Red Toryism.

1

I remember quite distinctly (as if it were yesterday) the animated conversations around our dinner table in the late 1950s when Claude Bissell had been appointed President of University of Toronto. Bissell was President of University of Toronto from 1956–1971, and he embodied a way of being (as did many others in the post-WW II era) in the next phase of the Canadian nationalist tradition. Bissell had been involved, when President of Carleton University (1956–1958), in coordinating a series of lectures that was published as *Our Living Tradition* (1957). Bissell stood, in many ways, on the solid and firm shoulders of the first Canadian born Governor General in Canada, Vincent Massey (1952–1959). Vincent Massey was George Grant's uncle, and the Massey Commission (1949–1951) was central in shaping and defining the way forward for Canada after WW II. George Grant was asked to contribute the article on "Philosophy" for the Massey Commission, and in the essay, he challenged the drift and direction of most forms of modern philosophy and called, prophet like, philosophers to return to a more ancient and contemplative approach to doing philosophy. Grant's article in the Massey Commission deeply offended the leading philosopher in Canada at the time (Fulton Anderson—Chair of Philosophy at University of Toronto), and Anderson (and other Canadian philosophers) organized their 1952 annual conference to debunk Grant (and those of his ilk). There can be no doubt, though, that with the Massey Commission a new form of mature Canadian nationalism was emerging in the post-WW II era in which Vincent Massey, Claude Bissell and George Grant were to take serious leadership in forging and making—this form of Canadian nationalism had a lingering attachment to the older tradition of England and was profoundly suspicious of the United States as an emerging empire. This way of thinking was, obviously, to play a significant role in *Lament for a Nation: The Defeat of Canadian Nationalism*.

The Liberal Party of Canada had dominated Canadian politics after WWII, and William Lyon MacKenzie King (the longest serving Canadian Prime Minister) and Louis St. Laurent guided the Liberal ship throughout most of the 1940s–1950s. King had a pronounced distaste for the English tradition and heritage (it had much to do with the way his prominent yet distant relative, William Lyon MacKenzie, was opposed by the more British oriented Family Compact in the 1837 Rebellion). King tended to turn to the USA as his north star, and Rockefeller and Roosevelt were his decided mentors. The fact that King was pro-USA and Massey doubted such an imperial turn meant that there were heated clashes between King and Massey. King, St. Laurent and C.D. Howe also played a significant role in hitching Canada's economic and military future to the USA. It was this typical annexationist or integrationist perspective of the historic liberal tradition in Canada that collided with those like Massey, Bissell and Grant.

Canada, in the 1940s–1950s, had been drawn into the gravitational field of the USA. Foreign investment amounted to 65%, manufacturing was 56% foreign owned, mining 60%, pulp and paper 80% and petroleum 90% foreign owned. It was this excessive dependence by Canada on, mostly, American ownership, that brought down, temporarily, the Liberal annexationist position (which Grant would eventually call—drawing from Alexandre Kojeve, see "Tyranny and Wisdom"—the universal and homogenous state). John Diefenbaker came to power in 1957 committed to retrieving a Canadian nationalist political position that was not beholden to the Americans. Prime Minister John Diefenbaker did not have the philosophic depth of Grant, but he dared to challenge, and for a few years (1957–1963), redirect Canadian domestic and foreign policy. Diefenbaker has been called a "Rogue Tory" (Denis Smith: *Rogue Tory: The Life and Legend of John G. Diefenbaker*, 1995), and there can be no doubt that Diefenbaker, in his imperfect and often erratic way, attempted to reclaim a form of conservatism in Canada

3

that challenged the powerful influence of liberalism in Canada and its various forms and guides in the USA. Diefenbaker's brand of conservatism was, in many ways, at the opposite end with the American republican tradition and had affinities with the National Policy of J.A. Macdonald and Disraeli. Diefenbaker, again and again, stood up to Kennedy, and Kennedy had no patience for Diefenbaker. The clashes and animosity between Kennedy and Diefenbaker are amply illustrated in Knowlton Nash's, *Kennedy and Diefenbaker: Fear and Loathing Across the Undefended Border* (1990).

The Federal election of 1963 in Canada was, largely, fought over whether Canada would take warheads for Bomarc missiles or whether Canada would refuse the American demands. Pearson bowed the knee to Kennedy and the Kennedy administration backed Pearson in the election. Diefenbaker refused to take warheads for the Bomarc missiles, he had opposed Kennedy on a variety of contentious issues before the election and his nationalist vision was held high in opposition to Pearsonian integrationism. Pearson won the 1963 election and with the defeat of Diefenbaker, Grant was convinced that a way of being Canadian was passing away. It was this death of an older notion of conservatism (of which the actual election was but a portal and metaphor) that Grant lamented in *Lament for a Nation: The Defeat of Canadian Nationalism*. The publication of *Lament* in 1965 became an immediate bestseller. The compact missive sold 7000 copies in the first six months and more than 50,000 copies in the next twenty-five years (William Christian: *George Grant: A Biography*, p. 279). The language of Red Toryism emerged in Canada with the publication of *Lament*, and to the structure and content of *Lament* I now turn.

Lament for a Nation

Lament for a Nation was, originally, written in seven chapters (seven being a sacred number) and in later editions (1970), Grant added an "Introduction" and in 1997 Sheila

Grant added an "Afterword". I will discuss both George and Sheila Grant's "Introduction" and "Afterword" after dealing with the main content of the original version of *Lament*.

Chapter I in *Lament for a Nation* is a frontal assault on all those who turned on Diefenbaker. The opening lines sum up Grant's passion well.

> Never has such a torrent of abuse been poured on any Canadian figure as that during the years from 1960 to 1965. Never have the wealthy and the clever been so united as they were in their joint attack on Mr. John Diefenbaker.

Grant turned on the liberal corporate and media power elite for maligning and defeating Diefenbaker. Grant uses two graphic illustrations to illuminate his poignant point. The life of a child is a good, and when a child dies, a legitimate lament is needful. Diefenbaker stood for something that was good in the Canadian historic way, his defeat and passing was like a death, hence a lament was in order. The second metaphor complements the tragic image of the death of a child. A fish survives within the reality of water—when the water is removed, the fish will die. The water that supported the fish (the ethos that supported the older Tory vision) has now been drained and many are like "gasping political fish".

Grant links the older conservative vision of Sir J.A. Macdonald to Diefenbaker's last stand contra Pearson in the 1963 election.

> We were grounded in the wisdom of Sir J.A. Macdonald who saw plainly more than a hundred years ago that the only threat to nationalism was from the South, not from across the sea.

There can be no doubt that Grant is holding high an Anglo-Canadian political vision in the above statement in contrast to an Anglo-American political perspective. The deeper meaning and significance of this will be unfolded, at the level of political philosophy, as Grant develops his argument in *Lament for a Nation*.

Grant brings to a brief conclusion a couple of main points in Chapter I. There were few in the early 1960s that dared to compare the USA to an empire—many do this today. Grant makes it quite explicit that the USA is an empire that is enfolded in certain principles and, equally so, Canadians are being drawn uncritically into the fold of such liberal principles and practices. The final lines of the chapter turn to Richard Hooker (Anglican Divine of the 16th century). Hooker's grounding in an older history in the midst of theological and political chaos had some affinities with Grant in the 1960s. The unpacking of the sentence from Hooker will, in many ways, be the core of *Lament*. "Posterity may know we have not loosely through silence permitted things to pass away as in a dream". Grant feared, with the coming to be of the American imperial way (and Canadian colonials and compradors serving such an agenda) that things that were once goods and held dear could "pass away as in a dream". Grant refused, in the passing, to be silent.

Chapter II in *Lament*, once again, turns to the liberal power elite and establishment in Canada and clarifies, in poignant and not to be forgotten detail, how and why such a ruling class became committed to a continentalist perspective. There are "conflicts over principles" in the defeat of Diefenbaker, and the Canadian liberal classes were pro-American, whereas Diefenbaker was torn between an Anglo-Canadian-American form of liberalism and a unique Anglo-Canadian Toryism (or, as Horowitz would call it, the "Tory touch"). The initial part of Chapter II describes, in a historic way, how Canadian liberals after WWII turned from England as their north star and turned to the USA as their master and mentor. This turn was philosophic, economic, military and political and the implications were obvious. The commitment by the liberal power elite hastened the further immersed Canadians into the ideology of American liberalism. Those with no memory merely assumed that American liberalism was the alpha and omega of political thought and action—Grant dared to question such an unthinking and uncritical position.

Grant was not an uncritical fan of Diefenbaker. Most of Chapter II makes it abundantly clear that Diefenbaker was pulled in inconsistent directions and this was his fault and failing. There was, in Diefenbaker, the older nationalist Tory vision that was suspicious of Anglo-American liberalism, but there was also the Anglo-Canadian-American liberalism that dwelt in Diefenbaker. It was this inner struggle as it worked itself out in Diefenbaker's life that led to his defeat. When push came to shove in the 1963 election, Diefenbaker held high the older Tory tradition contra Kennedy-Pearson against both those in his party and in the Liberal party. Pearson was much more the predictable Canadian liberal who fawned at the feet of the ideology of liberalism and the embodiment of such a position in Kennedy. Grant dissected, in the bulk of Chapter II, how Diefenbaker's inconsistencies and glaring mistakes led to his defeat. Grant did, therefore, like many, challenge and criticise Diefenbaker, but he thought that Diefenbaker was pointer and cairn to an older way of being Canadian.

If Chapter II in *Lament for a Nation* probes the way Diefenbaker was torn between liberalism and a more classic form of nationalist conservatism, Chapter III is a spirited and animated defence of Diefenbaker and Howard Green's (Minister of External Affairs) nationalism. Canada had a history of being rooted in the English way, and as Canada became more independent, the task was to find a middle way between the waning of the British empire and the waxing of the American empire. The Cuban Missile Crisis of 1962 and the Federal election of 1963 (which was about warheads for Bomarc missiles being placed on Canadian soil) raised the question of Canadian identity. The problem, as Grant rightly noted, was this: The English had, since WWI (and more since WWII) turned to the USA as their north star. The power centre was, increasingly so, the USA, NATO and NORAD (American military organizations). The less important and more conciliar idea of the British Commonwealth had become secondary to British foreign policy. Diefenbaker and Green were still committed to an older notion of the commonwealth rather than American unilateralism.

Grant saw in the post-WWII emergence of the American empire the continuation of Jeffersonian liberalism: will (power), liberty and reason were at the core of such a creed and the American empire of Kennedy embodied such a reality. The fact that C.D. Howe and William Lyon MacKenzie had prepared Canadians well to accept such a vision and Pearson merely oiled the wheels of such a continentalist approach was at the core of Grant's concerns. Were there options to this worrisome integration of willing, liberty and reason? The fact that Green and Diefenbaker (Green more than Diefenbaker) dared to oppose the liberal alliance of Kennedy-Pearson raised the question about the grounds for doing so. Did Green and Diefenbaker think from a counter tradition that saw through the pretences and rhetoric of liberalism? What did they see that most did not see? Was the Jeffersonian liberalism that Kennedy and Pearson espoused more about liberty for the powerful than about a form of liberty that was an extension of the good? Certainly, the liberal tradition of Locke and Jefferson (of which Kennedy and Pearson imbibed) had turned their backs on an older form of conservatism. The 1962 Cuban Missile Crisis and the 1963 Federal election were, for Grant, about more than merely a military and economic clash of interests—they reflected and embodied two different ways of understanding what it meant to be human, political and Canadian—there was, in fact, a parting of ideological paths. Grant was convinced that in the 1963 election more than Diefenbaker was defeated—in fact, an older notion of the political good had been defeated and died.

Chapters I–III in *Lament for a Nation* dealt, mostly, with the political events of post-WWII Canada and the

Canadian turn to the liberal USA and away from an older English conservatism. It is important to note, of course, as I mentioned above, that English liberalism was the founding political philosophy of the USA and played a significant role in the origins of Canada, also. So, when Grant turned to an alternate political vision, he was calling forth a counter tradition that had almost been forgotten and vanished as the hegemony of liberalism came to dominate English speaking Canada. Chapter IV begins, in a more focussed and definite manner, to clarify the nature of liberalism as a form of political theory and how such an imperial ideology has muted an older Anglo-Canadian Toryism.

Chapters IV–VI in **Lament** walk the reader into the centre and core of Grant doing political philosophy at a high level. The Anglo-American-Canadian liberal tradition is unpacked and unfurled both in underlying principles and content. Most of the mainstream liberal theorists and activists are brought on historic front stage for one and all to see as they act out their parts in England and North America. Grant's clear and poignant probes of both the appeal and imperial nature of liberalism are clearly articulated and enucleated. The crude and subtler forms of liberalism that, like roots in a tree, hold the truck and tree up yet often remain invisible, are unfolded in thought and deed. Grant also makes it clear what a historic Toryism is when compared with various forms of Canadian and American conservatism. The High Tory line and lineage of Coleridge, Johnson, Swift and Hooker are held high, and Grant does not flinch from placing Burke in the Whig camp (most American conservatives turn to Burke as their mascot and bearer of the conservative way). Grant was much too grounded in history and in an older understanding of Toryism to doff the cap to Burke and tribe. The fact that Grant, rightly so, placed Edmund Burke in the liberal clan meant he had many an affinity with the much respected leftist political philosopher, C. B. Macpherson, who also argued that Burke was a Rockingham Whig.

Chapter IV pondered and dissected the Canadian Liberal Party and liberal establishment, insisting that liberalism had become the dominant political philosophy in Canada. The option to such a political Sanhedrin was Leftist Castroism and French nationalist Gaullism—both forms of political thought were willing to use the state for the common good of citizens—both forms, in short, of leftist statism had much in common with High Toryism. The American conservative and republican idea that a lighter and minimal state is best ran contrary to the Anglo-Canadian High Tory notion that a strong state, at its best, exists to ensure, in an organic manner, that all citizens within the state are guaranteed basic goods necessary for a civilized existence. Chapter V further unpacked the complex nature of social and entrepreneurial liberalism. The level of philosophic depth and detail that Grant goes into in his various and varied probes of liberalism in Chapters IV–V prepare the reader well for his investigation of the history of French and English High Toryism in Chapter VI. Chapter VI is truly the must read chapter in *Lament* both for an understanding of historic Toryism and why Grant thought such a way of being, in an age of progress, was an impossibility. The dynamo of liberal principles had won the day, and Hegel sat on the victor's throne. This did not mean, though, Grant took a defeatist view—like a prophet of old, he both lamented yet pointed, in a creative and constructive way to other, older possibilities. Chapter VI points the way to Grant's more complex argument in Chapter VII about "necessity" and the "good" which many readers simply ignore in their appropriation of *Lament for a Nation.*

Grant and Red Toryism

When **Lament for a Nation** left the publishing tarmac in 1965 many was the conservative that was startled by Grant's position. The Blue Tories in Canada (classical economic liberals) insisted Grant was not one of them. The New Left thought Grant's form of nationalist Toryism had many an affinity with their agenda. Gad Horowitz coined the term "Red Tory", and he applied it to Grant after reading *Lament*. Horowitz and Grant engaged in many a public dialogue about the use of "Red Tory", and Grant was always suspicious about the term being applied to him. The New Left in the 1960s (of which Horowitz was a comrade) were both nationalist and socialist—Grant had nationalist leanings, but he was not a socialist—he was committed to the lived tension of state and society working together for the common good—the New Left socialists leaned more in a strong statist direction. Red was the colour, of course, of the socialist left and Grant had his doubts about the secular socialist Left. The historic High Tory tradition is certainly not secular nor is it socialist—there seemed to be affinities between the New Left and High Tories, but Grant made it clear, again and again, he was not a Red Tory in the sense in which Horowitz and the New Left understood Red Tory. Grant was, in most ways, a High Tory which most in the New Left lacked the historic depth to comprehend. The "Tory touch" that, Horowitz suggested, made Canada different from the USA, was not, as Horowitz thought and argued, a red tory touch—it was more High Toryism—much more nuanced than the ideology of Red Toryism.

The ongoing debate and dialogue about Canadian Red Toryism, Horowitz and Grant, misreads of both of them and the ongoing interest in Red Toryism have certainly not ended. *Lament for a Nation* brought to the fore a unique and distinctive Canadian way of understanding the political good that did not rest easily with either the right or left, conservative of liberal political ideologies. It was Grant who unearthed this older Anglo-Canadian Tory tradition in the 1960s, but Grant realized, only so well, that he stood on the shoulders of many who had gone before him.

LAMENT FOR A NATION:
A JEREMIAD FOR OUR TIMES

Lament for a Nation should be respected as a masterpiece of political meditation. – Peter Emberley

Masterpiece is not a word to use lightly, but *Lament for a Nation* merits it. – William Christian

It is fifty years ago (1965–2015) since George Grant's **Lament for a Nation: The Defeat of Canadian Nationalism** took wings and left the press. It is most appropriate, therefore, to reflect on this timely text and meditate on its perennial relevance for Canadian thought and political life.

There is no doubt that **Lament for a Nation** is a compact and succinct masterpiece. It says much in a few pages. It is very much a tract for the times. Alex Colville, the well known Canadian painter, called **Lament for a Nation**, a political novel. When this missive was published, the arguments in it awoke and stirred many in the New Left and Counter Culture in Canada to fight for what Grant seemed to think was passing away. **Lament for a Nation** has appealed to many audiences for many different reasons, but the truths in it are as relevant today in an age of globalization and a 9-11 imperial world as they were in 1965. What, then, are the ideas and arguments in **Lament for a Nation**, and what can they still speak and say to us?

The 1963 Federal election in Canada set the stage for **Lament for a Nation**. Tommy Douglas (NDP) joined ranks with Lester Pearson (Liberals) to defeat John Diefenbaker (Progressive Conservatives). Grant had pleaded with Douglas not to side with Pearson. President Kennedy had backed Pearson, and Grant knew that if Douglas tipped his cap to Pearson, this signaled a green light to Kennedy's brand of American imperialism and the defeat of Canadian nationalism. Kennedy despised Diefenbaker, and although Grant was no uncritical fan of Diefenbaker, he did stand by his nationalism against American imperialism.

Chapter I of *Lament for a Nation* is a rapid overview of the liberal pack of wolves (academics, journalists, politicians, business leaders) who turned on Diefenbaker. The opening lines begin like this: "Never has such a torrent of abuse been poured on any Canadian figure as that during the years from 1960 to 1965. Never have the wealthy and the clever been so united as they were in their joint attack on Mr. John Diefenbaker". The turn from Diefenbaker to Pearson-Kennedy was a turn from a unique and indigenous Canadian nationalist way to the American liberal and imperial way. Grant laments this choice by Canadians. He laments this fact as a parent would the death of a child that was most loved. Life will go on, of course, but something is lost in the passing of what was loved and cared for, something that offered life and hope. Diefenbaker offered such a nationalist hope, but Canadians would have none of it. Most preferred Kennedy's Camelot to the True North. A vision was being lost, also, and Chapter I ends with the opening lines of Hooker's (16th century Anglican theologian) *Laws of Ecclesiastical Polity:* "Posterity may know we have not loosely through silence permitted things to pass away as in a dream". There is more to Grant's lament than merely the passing away of Canadian nationalism, but in the early chapters of *Lament for a Nation* this is the main motif. Grant did not want things to pass away as in a dream.

Chapter II takes Diefenbaker to task. Grant was no uncritical fan of Diefenbaker, and in Chapter II of *Lament for a Nation* he clearly and succinctly summarizes many and most of Diefenbaker's foibles and failings, and they were many. Grant does point out, though, Diefenbaker had inherited a Canada from William Lyon Mackenzie King, C.D. Howe and Louis St. Laurent that had become a colony and branch plant of the USA. Diefenbaker had to do battle both with those in the Progressive Conservative party that longed for integration with the USA and with the Liberal party. In short, he had a rather significant battle to fight on a variety of fronts.

How did Diefenbaker conceive Canada? Why did the men who run the country come to dislike and then fear his conception? The answers demonstrate much about Canada and its collapse. It is these sorts of questions and answers to them that Grant probes. Chapter II makes it clear that the questions raised about the fate and future of Canada are complex, and Diefenbaker, in an imperfect way attempted to answer such questions in a nationalist way that challenged Kennedy, the USA and the Canadian colonialism of Pearson and Douglas.

If Chapter II in *Lament for a Nation* highlights the fumbling, errors and blunders of Diefenbaker, then Chapter III clearly articulates that Diefenbaker was a man of principle, and he was toppled for such nationalist principles. The 1963 election was fought on the issue of whether Canada would take warheads for Bomarc missiles. Pearson, following Kennedy, said we should and would. Diefenbaker, much to the anger and chagrin of many in his party, said a defiant and firm No to Kennedy's orders. This was just the tip of the iceberg, though. Diefenbaker had, again and again, opposed and thwarted Kennedy's plans for Canada. Diefenbaker had questioned the way Kennedy had handled the Cuban missile crisis, he had initiated trade ties with Cuba and China when Kennedy had put a trade embargo on them, and he refused to join the Organization of American States (a front for American interests in Latin America). In short, Diefenbaker, as a conservative, locked horns with Kennedy's liberalism each step of the way. Grant makes all this quite clear. If Diefenbaker had merely wanted power, he would, like Pearson, have dutifully genuflected to Kennedy. He didn't, and he paid the price for doing so. "The defence crises of 1962 and 1963 revealed the depth of Diefenbaker's nationalism". It was in these years that Canadian nationalism was tested and found wanting. Canadians turned to the USA as their great good place, and Diefenbaker did his best to warn Canadians that such a Trojan horse could and would overwhelm the Canadian way. Chapter III is a spirited and animated defence of Howard Green (who Grant has much affinity with) and Diefenbaker. Diefenbaker was a tragic hero, but he was a hero nonetheless. Grant walks the extra mile to make this quite clear for those who only can see Diefenbaker in a negative way.

Chapter IV opens with these words: "in the light of Diefenbaker, I would like to turn to the Canadian establishment and its political instrument, the Liberal party". The rest of the chapter tells the tale of how the liberal vision of Canada, at essence and at core, is one with the liberal vision of the USA. The Liberal party sees itself as the bearer of such a liberal and progressive vision, and most liberals see the future and fate of Canada as being one and the same (on most major issues) as the USA. Grant makes clear how this annexationist and continentalist vision has been brokered and furthered by the Liberal Party of Pearson-St. Laurent-King-Laurier and tribe. This, in short, is the Canadian establishment, and these are their aims and goals for Canada. A quote from E.P. Taylor sums things up quite nicely: "Canadian nationalism! How old-fashioned can you get?"

Grant points out that there were two ways of opposing the liberal integrationist vision with the USA: Castro and Cuba and De Gaulle and France. Canada was not likely to follow Cuba, but the Gaullist tradition had some affinities with Sir J.A. Macdonald's idea for the True North. But, since the capitalist class in Canada are more American than Canadian nationalist, the Gaullist tradition has as much chance of taking the lead in Canada as does Castro's experiment in Cuba. It is the Liberal party that has assumed liberalism is the only political philosophy worth bending the knee to, and it is this creed and dogma that liberals see themselves as making sure all Canadians live by. Were there other options to the ideology of liberalism and the formal politics of the Liberal party that could point the way to alternate pathways other than the inevitable fate of liberalism? Are we indeed at the end of both history and ideology?

Chapter V moves the discussion from the many actors and actresses who play their roles on the stage of history to the ideas and ideologies that are the script and cue for such political thespians. Chapter V moves **Lament for a Nation** to a deeper, more demanding place. "The confused strivings of politicians, businessmen, and civil servants cannot alone account for Canada's collapse. This stems from the very character of the modern era". It is at this point that we can see that there is much more at work in Grant's argument than merely a lament for Canadian nationalism. The lament goes much deeper.

Grant sees the modern era and ethos as dominated by liberalism. This liberal creed and dogma emerged in the Reformation (as Grant made clear in his earlier book, **Philosophy and the Mass Age**). The deeper lament is about the passing away of the tradition of the Ancients and the coming to be of the Moderns. Plato and Aristotle, Augustine and Hooker, Swift and Coleridge had notions of the self and society, of human nature and the good life that stood in opposition to those like Locke and Hobbes, Paine and Jefferson. Grant makes plain the aim of this chapter: "I must turn away from Canadian history to the more important questions of political theory". It is in this pivotal chapter that Grant makes clear why he sides with the Ancients rather than the Modern way, and why he sees the individualist and first generation liberalism of Locke, Hobbes, Hume and Smith and the social and second generation liberalism of Rousseau, Kant and Hegel as kissing cousins. First and second generation liberals do disagree about the role of the state in bringing about the good of the individual and society, but both agree that liberty, equality, choice, and freedom are the core of the liberal way. The debate between first and second generation liberals is not so much about the principles and premises of liberalism but more about the accessibility and implementation of such principles for one and all. Grant makes it clear that such principles are problematic, and, if unquestioned, lead to serious problems. Grant, more than any other modern Canadian political philosopher, has dared to ask questions about the matrix of liberalism. Chapter V in *Lament for a Nation* is a sustained reflection on the inadequacy of liberal principles. If liberalism is flawed at the core and centre, what is the Tory alternate?

Chapter VI takes a long and hard look at the roots of Canadian conservatism. Grant makes it quite clear that the problem with a great deal of Canadian English speaking political thought is that it has been shaped by English liberalism. Canada was formed by many who came from England who had affinities with Locke and Smith, Hume and Hobbes. The older and more organic tradition of Hooker and Coleridge was waning at the time in England when Canada was being founded. This means Canada, like the USA, shares a certain liberal ethos. But, Canada, unlike the USA, still had a memory of an older, more ordered tradition with an abiding concern for the commonweal. It is this tension in the DNA and genetic code of English speaking Canada that makes Canada quite different from the liberty loving Yankees to the south. Canada, also, unlike the USA, walked the extra mile to preserve the French way of life. Many of the French who settled in Quebec (and elsewhere in Canada) had opposed the French Revolution of 1789. This meant that they, like the older English High Tories, shared a certain view of the good and just life. The English Tories and French Conservatives may have differed on some points, but both agreed that they did not want to be liberals or Americans.

The conservative tradition in Canadian, therefore, brought together the French and English, to oppose American liberal ideals and American imperialism. Grant makes it clear in Chapter VI that the English in Canada, for the most part, have forgotten their older Tory ties. He does suggest, though, that the French are much closer to an older notion of conservatism. The roots of Canadian conservatism (English and French) are much older and go much deeper into the Western Classical tradition of thought, culture and political theory than does modern liberalism (which finds its fullest expression and embodiment in the USA). Grant is ready to concede that there can be some protest to bourgeois liberalism, but even this can be co-opted by those in power. Grant had, in the 1960s, supported many in the New Left and Counter Culture. He stood by the side of the New Left and the Counter Culture in their criticisms of the Canadian and American liberal bourgeois ethos. But, he had this to say as a form of warning:

> The enormity of the break from the past will arouse in the dispossessed youth intense forms of beatness. But, after all, the United States supports a large Beat fringe. Joan Baez and Pete Seeger titillate the status quo rather than threaten it. Dissent is built into the fabric of the modern system. We bureaucratize it as much as anything else. Is there any reason to believe French Canada will be any different? A majority of the young is patterned for its place in the bureaucracies. Those who resist such shaping will retreat into a fringe world of pseudo-revolt.

The Beats, therefore, might seem to be questioning the status quo, but it is their anarchist fringe world and pseudo-revolt mentality (grounded and rooted in liberal notions of liberty and individualism) that makes them most American and easily co-opted. This is why Grant, at day's end, speaks a firm and solid No to the USA in either its liberal bourgeois or Beat protest form: he saw them as different sides of the same liberal coin. At a fundamental level, therefore, Grant disagreed with the political philosophy of liberalism, and he thought the USA incarnated such a liberal tradition more than any other state in the world. In short, Grant recognized that there are those who think we have come to the end of history and ideology, but he still can envision another way.

Grant is only too well aware, though, that the forces and ideology of liberalism (as embodied in the USA and bowed before by Canadian colonials and compradors) seems to be the necessary fate we must all, whether we like it or not, live with. Is this, then, our fate? Are we doomed and fated to be liberals, and is history (in terms of ideological battles) over and done? How are we to live if liberalism is both our necessity and determined fate?

Chapter VII concludes this tract for the times. Chapters I–IV dealt with Canadian history, political actors and party politics. Chapters V–VI walked the reader into the area of political philosophy and theory. It is from the realm of theory that the script is given to the actors who merely read their parts in time. Grant questions, in these chapters, whether the script, itself, might have some problems. Could the lines of liberalism, the play and drama be written differently? Many don't think so, and most oppose any fiddling or altering with the script and text of liberalism. Chapter VII has a more theological bent and orientation to it than the other chapters. Grant makes it clear in Chapter VII that Hegel and his notion of history is the crown jewel and centre piece of liberalism. Hegel had argued that liberalism fulfilled the deepest longing of the human intellectual and political journey: God and liberalism are One. Liberalism is, almost, in Hegel, divinely inspired and ordained. If this is the case, and liberalism is the creed of the day that cannot be questioned or doubted, then it is our fate that we must work within the matrix of the liberal framework. But, Grant asks, is fate and necessity the same as the Good? The Classical Tradition of the Good stands in a questioning and interrogating opposition to liberalism. Chapter VII ends with this question, therefore. "Liberalism was, in origin, criticism of the old established order. Today it is the voice of the establishment". Grant set himself the task of questioning both liberal ideology and the establishment class that defined and defended it. This made him, in some ways, an uncomfortable prophet, and *Lament for a Nation* a tract with many a parallel to the Jewish prophet Jeremiah who wrote *Lamentations*. Grant attempts to evoke notions of the Good, he points the way to such places and he wonders, while

19

doing so, whether there will ever be a turn to such a way? If liberalism is our fate, then the Good might just be eclipsed.

Is Grant a cynic and skeptic, therefore? Does he see no possibility of opposing and resisting the Moloch, establishment and matrix of liberalism? Grant was asked in 1970 to write an "Introduction" to *Lament for a Nation;* he did so. It is in this "Introduction" that he attempted to state his case against apathy, cynicism, indifference and skepticism. It is interesting to note that in the "Introduction" he refers twice to the Moloch of the USA. This was a term that was used by Allen Ginsberg in his classic poem, *Howl* (1956). There are close connections between Ginsberg and Grant in what they are protesting against. Ginsberg's *Howl* and Grant's *Lament* do share some important affinities, and these do need to be explored. *Lament for a Nation* is, in many ways, the Canadian version of *Howl.* The fact that Grant uses the image and metaphor of Molech as a way of depicting the American empire in his "Introduction" to *Lament for a Nation* highlighted his affinity with the New Left and the Counter Culture of the 1960s and the 1970s, but, as I noted above, Grant was somewhat wary of the fringe world and pseudo-revolt of the Counter Culture. Those like Ginsberg and clan used and furthered the very principles of liberalism in their legitimate criticisms of the liberal bourgeois culture that the dominant classes in the USA sought to defend.

Grant was neither a cynic nor pessimist, though. He insisted and argued in his "Introduction" that action was better than apathy, and political paralysis is not the answer. Liberalism might dominate (in a variety of guises and appearances), but if history teaches nothing else it is that all ideologies have their day. When such a day will come is beyond the ken of most, but to sit down and fold the hands is not the answer. Grant ever pointed to the Good, and encouraged one and all to look where his finger was pointing. The language of optimism and pessimism must be set within a much larger and longer historic context. When this is done, and the end of the journey is seen, there is reason for hope and Grant was ever hopeful.

Sheila Grant (George Grant's wife) was asked to write an

"Afterword" to *Lament for a Nation* in 1997. She made it clear that if *Lament for a Nation* is ever going to be properly understood, a better reading and understanding of Chapter VII is much needed. Sheila further unpacked Grant's discussion about necessity and the Good, and argued that Grant was not a pessimist. He believed in acting even when the odds seemed overwhelming, and he lived from a source that went much deeper and was much older than liberalism. The final few paragraphs in Chapter VII highlight what this source was and why Grant turned to such a well to dip his bucket.

There is no doubt *Lament for a Nation* is a political masterpiece and a missive of prophetic vigour and depth. This tract for the times moves from the Federal election of 1963, to Canadian-American relations, to political philosophy, to theology and back, in the 1970 "Introduction", to Canadian-American relations and the need for Canadians to be ever vigilant about American intentions and the colonial class in Canada that would make Americans of Canadians.

Lament for a Nation has many affinities with Ginsberg's *Howl*, but even though Grant might lament and Ginsberg howl at the imperial nature of the USA and the liberal bourgeois ethos that underwrites such a military industrial complex, Grant would see Ginsberg, the New Left, the Beats and the Counter Culture of the 1960s and 1970s as more subtle agents of the liberal ideology that he sought to question and interrogate. In fact, a close reading of life and writings of Allen Ginsberg and George Grant would highlight how and why the Canadian High Tory way shares some affinities with the Anarchist Left, but, on substantive issues, they part company on both the issues of philosophic principles and political means. George Grant gives Canadians a uniquely Canadian way (both in a philosophical and political way) of opposing the varieties of liberalism that are smuggled into Canada, like a Trojan horse, by Americans. Beware, indeed, of Americans when they come bringing gifts of either the imperial, liberal bourgeois or protest type. To quote another Canadian, by way of conclusion, "even the dissidents speak as members of the empire" (John Newlove).

21

ALLEN GINSBERG AND GEORGE GRANT: HOWL AND LAMENT FOR A NATION

It is fifty years this autumn since the Beat Movement was launched at *Six Gallery* in San Francisco (October 13, 1955). Some of the American Beats from the East Coast (Jack Kerouac and Allen Ginsberg) and the West Coast (Kenneth Rexroth, Gary Snyder, Philip Whalen, Lawrence Ferlinghetti) met and read together at this gathering. John Suiter rightly says, "The *Six Gallery* reading has sometimes been called the first synthesis of the East and West Coast factions of the Beat Generation" (p.148).

Kenneth Rexroth had hiked to many of the peaks in the North Cascades in the 1920s. His rambling and tramping tales are well told in *An Autobiographical Novel* (ch. 30). Gary Snyder worked on lookout peaks (Crater and Sourdough Mountains) in 1952–1953, but he could not get work in the North Cascades in 1954 because of his affiliations with unions and anarchist left groups. These were the McCarthy years, and Snyder was a victim of such a red scare. Philip Whalen worked on lookout peaks (Sauk and Sourdough Mountains) in 1953–1955. Jack Kerouac, a year after the *Six Gallery* reading (1956), spent a summer on Desolation Peak in the North Cascades. *The Dharma Bums* (1958), *Lonesome Traveler* (1960) and *Desolation Angels* (1965) all reflect much of what he saw and experienced on Desolation Peak.

The *Six Gallery* reading of 1955 was, therefore, a pivotal event in bringing together the ecological Beats of the West Coast and the Bop and Beat tradition of the East Coast. Allen Ginsberg attended and participated in the *Six Gallery* reading, and a year later, *Howl and Other Poems* was published. The back cover of *Howl*, from City Lights Books, says

Allen Ginsberg's *Howl and Other Poems* was originally published by City Lights Books in the Fall of 1956. Subsequently seized by the U.S. Customs and the San Francisco police, it was the subject of a long court

22

trial at which a series of poets and professors persuaded the courts that the book was not obscene. Over 30,000 copies have since been sold.

There is no doubt *Howl* created a commotion and stir in the San Francisco area at the time.

Forty years have passed since George Grant's *Lament for a Nation* (1965) was published. *Lament for a Nation*, like *Howl*, created strong reactions. Many in the New Left and Counter-culture in Canada were drawn to *Lament for a Nation*. Many in the political centre and political right in Canada were offended by what Grant was saying in *Lament*. Grant was fully aware of what he was saying and doing at the time, and he knew that his criticisms of the American empire (and the Canadian colonial and comprador class) would not be taken well by the ruling establishment and high mucky-mucks at the time.

Lament has been called "a masterpiece of political meditation", and Darrol Bryant sees it as a tract for the times that stands within the Old Testament prophetic tradition of *Lamentations*. Kenneth Rexroth has argued, in defending Ginsberg, his poetry stands "in the long Jewish Old Testament tradition of testimonial poetry". It is significant to note that Grant in his 1970 "Introduction" to *Lament for a Nation* refers twice to the image and metaphor of Molech. Molech was seen by the Jewish people as a devouring god that consumed and destroyed the life of one and all. Molech is a central metaphor in Part II of *Howl*. Grant also refers to the Beats and the Counter-culture in *Lament for a Nation*. Ginsberg and Grant seem, at first glance, to be lamenting and howling against the same Molech. The American empire seemed to consume one and all. The best and the brightest did their best to oppose and resist such a monster and leviathan, but souls and bodies were required to feed the ravenous appetite of such a beast. Was it possible to live a meaningful life without bowing and genuflecting to Molech?

Howl and *Lament for a Nation* seem to be on the same page and fighting the same enemy and opponent. But are they? Ginsberg and Grant do agree on what they want to be free from. Do they agree on what they want to be free for? It is by understanding this difference that we will understand the different paths taken between American anarchism (and Canadian devotees of such a tradition) and Canadian High Tory nationalism. The different paths hiked do lead to quite distinctly different places on the political spectrum. Let us, all too briefly, light and linger at *Howl* and *Lament for a Nation* to see how and why American anarchism and Canadian nationalism, although seeming to have much in common at one level, have less and less in common at more substantive levels.

It is significant to note, by way of beginning, to mention who *Howl* and *Lament for a Nation* are dedicated to. Ginsberg offers up *Howl* to Jack Kerouac, William Burroughs and Neal Cassady; all three were East Coast Bop and Beat poets and activists. *Howl* was written for Carl Solomon, and William Carlos Williams wrote the introduction. Kerouac is very much in the lead in the dedication, and Ginsberg says, "Several phrases and the title of *Howl* are taken from him". We need to ask ourselves this simple question if we ever hope to get a fix and feel for Ginsberg's drift and direction: what is the essence and core of the East Coast Bop and Beat ethos, and how did Ginsberg, Kerouac, Burroughs, Cassady, Williams and Solomon embody such an ideology? There tends to be six distinct points to be noted here: i) individual feelings and emotions are paramount—reason and one-dimensional science are the problem, ii) protest and rebellion against the American empire and Puritanism are dominant, iii) uprootedness and unrootedness are welcomed—being on the road becomes a new creed and dogma, iv) eclectic spirituality becomes the new sacrament—a rather raw sexuality and spirituality are fused, v) institutions—whether they are religious, political, cultural, economic—are seen as the problem, and vi) anarchism is seen as the liberating way in opposition to the authoritarian and repressive nature of all ideologies and institutions.

Liberty tends to trump order, individuality repels the common good, equality of desires is held high, raw experience banishes the wisdom of tradition, and spirituality is freed from the bondage of shackles of religious dogmas and institutions. Needless to say, such a position becomes its own ideology, creed and institution that cannot be doubted and must be defended at all costs by its guardians and gatekeepers.

There is no doubt that Kerouac, Burroughs and Cassady embodied such a vision. Carolyn Cassady dared to expose and question such an ideology in *Off the Road: My Years with Cassady, Kerouac and Ginsberg* (1990). Even Kerouac was beginning to ask substantive questions about the Beats and distance himself from them in the early 1960s. He makes this quite clear in *Lonesome Traveler* (1960) when he said, "I am actually not *Beat* but a strange solitary crazy Catholic mystic", and with the publication of *Vanity of Duluoz* (1968), Kerouac made it clear that much of the Bop and Beat tradition was much more about a rather inflated vanity and egoistic and indulgent individualism than anything else. But Kerouac still remained the liberty-loving and solitary Catholic mystic. The American DNA and genetic code of individualism was still his master and guru.

Grant dedicated *Lament for a Nation* "To Derek Bedson and Judith Robinson: Two Lovers Of Their Country: One Living and One Dead". Who were Derek Bedson and Judith Robinson, and how, as Canadian lovers of their country, were they different from Kerouac, Burroughs and Cassady? Derek Bedson, unlike many of the Beats, had a strong commitment to the Anglican High Tory tradition both in politics and religion. He was active in the Anglican Church of Canada (ever the gadfly to its emerging liberalism) and he worked in the area of both federal and provincial politics. Bedson, unlike the Beats, realized that both political and religious institutions (although always imperfect), were

25

important means to work within for the common good of the nation and the people. Society and the state (both have their distortions and demons) when understood aright should and can work together, in an organic, just, and ordered way, for the commonweal.

The philosophic tradition of liberalism, in either its American imperial form or its Beat reactionary form, was about individuals using their liberty in a unilateral way to undermine and deconstruct those things that, as people, we share in common. Grant turned to Bedson as a true teacher and mentor who loved his country. Judith Robinson was a feisty and fiery Red Tory who, as an animated journalist, challenged both liberalism and the Liberal party in Canada. In fact, her relentless assaults on the Liberal party led to the Royal Canadian Military Police (RCMP) bloodhounds being turned on her in the 1950s. Robinson thought the liberals were selling out Canada to the USA, and she would have none of it. The Liberal party of St. Laurent and King were an anathema to her. The American way (both in principle and fact) were something she had little or no patience for. George Grant, therefore, when he dedicated *Lament for a Nation* to Derek Bedson and Judith Robinson knew what he was doing and saying.

Many Canadians have, I suspect, heard of Ginsberg, Kerouac, Cassady, Williams and Burroughs. I question whether many have heard of Judith Robinson or Derek Bedson. What does this tell us about our Canadian soul and how it has been colonized by the American matrix?

There is little doubt that Bedson, Robinson and Grant stood in a very different place on the political and personal spectrum than Kerouac, Burroughs, Cassady and Ginsberg. Both clans could agree that American imperialism, corporate capitalism, consumerism, liberal bourgeois thought and Puritanism needed to be exposed and undressed. There was no depth to them. They embodied Nietzsche's "Last Man" or Miller's "Wrong Dream". Surely there was more to the good life than defining and defending personal peace and happiness. In short, Canadian High Tories and American Anarchist Beats do agree on the fact the patient is ill and ailing. They have much in common in their diagnosis. But they have quite a different way of healing the failing and faltering patient. The prognosis takes Grant and Ginsberg down different paths and to different places. What then is this different prognosis? Let us turn to *Howl* and *Lament for a Nation* to see what is seen. It is in this different seeing we will come to understand some important differences at a root, core and genetic, philosophic and practical level between Americans and Canadians.

It is fifty years since *Howl* was published. It is forty years since *Lament for a Nation* was published. It is at such remembering points we are offered the opportunity to see again what animates and tends to define the True North from the empire to the south.

Howl is divided into three sections and a "Footnote to Howl". Section I opens with the memorable lines that none forget once heard and read: "I saw the best minds of my generation destroyed by madness". The rest of the section is a prose-poem that describes how these best minds were destroyed, and equally so, how the artistic and visionary nature of such minds were bent and broken on the anvil of the modern world. Section I is both tragic and sad, and the ruined and wrecked lives are amply laid out for all to see in the most graphic and poignant of ways. We might ask, as we read Section I, whether these are the best minds (given their end points), but Ginsberg has told us these are the best and the brightest, so we heed and hear.

Section II turns, in a penetrating manner, to the place that has savaged such minds, and the potent image that speaks of such an alluring and tempting place: Molech, Molech and Molech becomes the destructive and dominant metaphor. The metaphor of Molech is unpacked and unraveled in a variety of ways, but there is no doubt that the best minds are defeated victims of Molech, and Molech will devour one and all. Who is Molech? Ginsberg makes this most clear. It is all forms of tyranny and authority that brutalize and are callous to the best minds. The USA is very much in the foreground, though.

Section III presses home the point in a more urgent and not to be forgotten manner. Section III is directed to Carl Solomon in Rockland. The political left is held high and idealized, and the USA is seen as the place of repression and destruction. The language is raw and graphic in *Howl*, and social reality is neatly and crisply divided into a rather simplistic either-or way of looking at things. "Footnote to Howl" walks the extra mile to shout from the rooftops the Holy, Holy, Holy theme: all is holy and needs to be seen as such. Ginsberg in this section is doing his best to fuse spirituality and sexuality, street life with city life. Nothing should be seen as unholy. All has goodness in and to it, and when this is seen, eternity is in our midst.

There are other poems in the *Howl* collection, also. "A Supermarket in California" doffs the cap to Walt Whitman, and "Transcription of Organ Music" takes the reader through and beyond the purpose of organ music. The transcription and the organ are meant to walk the attentive and alert to higher and deeper spiritual states. This poem points the way to what such a fusion of spirituality and sensuality might look like. "Sunflower Sutra" tells the tale of Ginsberg and Kerouac as they see, through Blake's sunflower, a sutra of insight in hard places. "America" is a longer poem, and true to form, turns on the USA. "In the Baggage Room at Greyhound", like other poems in the collection, takes the reader into the underground and underbelly of America. "An Asphodel", "Song", "Wild Orphan" and "In Back of the Real" close off this final section in *Howl and Other Poems*.

It must be remembered that these poems were published in 1956. The USA was in the thick of the Cold War, and anyone with the mildest sympathies with the left was seen as communist. The raw sexual and sensual language that permeates and pervades most of *Howl and Other Poems* is a frontal assault and attack on both middle class bourgeois America and the Puritan ethos that shaped such an ideology.

Ginsberg, in short, was pulling no punches. He thought the best minds in American had been driven mad by combination of the military industrial complex, anti-communist thinking and Puritan and bourgeois ethics. He howled against such a repressive way of being, and the state and police turned on him for doing so. *Howl* (1956) and *On the Road* (1955) became sacred texts and Bibles for the Beat generation, and Ginsberg became a high priest to such a generation with his fusion of sensuality-spirituality, anarchist-protest politics and a raw and in your face assault on middle class values. *Howl* became a lightning rod missive for those who felt ill at ease with expectations laid on them they had no interest in. Ginsberg's *Howl* spoke what many felt but had not yet put to words.

What are the points of concord and convergence between Grant's *Lament for a Nation* and Ginsberg's *Howl*, and equally important, what are the points of discord and divergence?

The 1965 edition of *Lament for a Nation* is divided into seven chapters. In some ways it is a prose-poem that deals with major political themes in Canada, and between Canada and the USA. George Grant added an "Introduction" in 1970, and Sheila Grant (George's wife) added an "Afterword" in 1997. I will stick with the 1965 edition of *Lament for a Nation*. I mentioned above that the very language of lament conjures up for the reader the tradition of Jewish political thought. The Jewish prophet Jeremiah wrote *Lamentations*. The fact that *Lament for a Nation* is divided into seven chapters reminds the reader of the seven days of creation in the Jewish tradition. The fact the seventh chapter is theological means that the political reflections have a deeper source than merely politics.

Chapter I in *Lament* deals with Diefenbaker's defeat by Pearson in the 1963 election. Grant saw this as a source of much concern, since Pearson was pro-American and Diefenbaker was a thorn in Kennedy's side. And, more worrisome for Grant, most Canadians were overjoyed to have

Pearson as the new Prime Minister of Canada. What did this say about Canadian nationalism?

Chapter II and III ponder both the follies and foolishness of Diefenbaker and his nobility and heroism. Grant was no uncritical fan of Diefenbaker, but he did think that Diefenbaker stood on principles, and his nationalist political principles brought about his demise. Chapter IV touches on both liberalism and the Liberal party in Canada, and why such a party has tended to dominate much of Canadian political life (and the consequences for Canadian nationalism).

Chapters V and VI, consciously so, walks the reader into the realms of political theory and political philosophy, and why at root and ground level, Canadian conservatism (in its English and French forms) is almost the opposite of American republican conservatism.

The fact that American liberalism (in its democratic and republican forms) seeks to dominate the world raises for Grant a worrisome question. Is there any way to oppose or resist this Molech? Is this, as Canadians, our fate and necessity? What can we do given this stubborn fact? Chapter VII opens up a dialogue about the difference between fate-necessity and the Good. How, as Canadians, can we live from something higher than what seems to be our dominant fate? Is it possible to get out of the matrix of American liberalism?

Lament for a Nation has been called a masterpiece, and it is for a variety of reasons. The tract for the times moves from the facts of Canadian and American political history, to Canadian and American political philosophy to theology. It is poignant and pungent prose writing in the best tradition of political pamphlets.

How, though, is **Lament for a Nation** similar and different from **Howl**, and what can these points of concord and discord tell us about the differences between Canadian and American thought and culture. There are five points of convergence, and five of divergence.

First, both **Lament** and **Howl** raise serious and substantive objections about the American military industrial complex, the power elite in the USA and the damage done by such an elite in various parts of the world.

Second, both write in an intense, committed and accessible manner. Ginsberg can be raw, crude and excessively graphic. Grant was much more polished, incisive and delicately evocative. Grant and Ginsberg do communicate through plain and direct speech, though, as participants in the tough issues of the time rather than as detached and cool-headed observers. Both are on the ice. Neither is in the balcony or bleachers.

Third, both men were critical of the liberal bourgeois tradition and a form of American Puritanism that justified such a smug view. Ginsberg rebelled against this by indulging all sorts of desires and interests, whereas Grant rebelled against the liberal bourgeois tradition by deepening and ordering his interests and desires towards the highest and noblest things. Both could agree that Locke's "life, liberty and estates" and Nietzsche's "last man" were something they did not want to be. They disagreed on the best path to hike when the Puritan-bourgeois-last man was left behind. Plato is quite different from Whitman, Coleridge from Blake. Grant was for the former, Ginsberg the latter. Allen Ginsberg sent me a couple of letters in the late 1980s (Jan. 1, 1989 and Feb. 6, 1989). The first discussed the Beats, his involvement with Naropa Institute, Buddhism, and Chogyam Trungpa Rinpoche and his rather negative and reactionary view of the Jewish God. The second letter was a copy of his small book on Blake (*Your Reason and Blake's System*). Both the long letter and the missive speak much about Ginsberg's commitments, and some of the distortions and caricatures he had of other traditions because of such commitments. Both Grant and Ginsberg rebelled against the American empire, Puritanism and the bourgeois tradition, but they turned to different wells to slake the thirst of their deeper longings and questions.

Fourth, both men are distinctively and consciously thinking from a religious and theological vision in more than merely a moral sense. Ginsberg begins *Howl* by saying "All

31

these books are published in Heaven", and Grant begins *Lament* by reference to Anglican parish life and ends with a sustained theological reflection on the difference between necessity-fate and the Good.

Fifth, neither Grant nor Ginsberg offer much of a way out of the problem. Ginsberg can howl and Grant can lament. This might be a good place to start, but it is hardly a positive, creative and constructive way to end. What lies on the far end and other side of howling and lamenting? There are, sadly so, many who begin and end in such a place.

If Grant and Ginsberg can meet and greet at this intersection place, where do they part paths and why? It is one thing to agree on what we oppose and desire to say a firm No to. It is quite another thing to state what we wish to affirm and say Yes to. There are many who often agree on what is not wanted, but such people often part paths when a serious discussion (at both a philosophical and practical level) begins on what is desired and wanted. This is where Ginsberg and Grant go in different directions. What are their points of discord and divergence, then?

First, Grant was Canadian, and he had a concern and commitment to Canadians and the way Canada is being colonized by the USA. Ginsberg was American, and he had little or no interest in the Canadian political tradition. *Lament for a Nation* deals with Canadian-American relations in a way *Howl* does not. When, as Canadians, we know more about Ginsberg than Grant, it speaks much about a way of being colonized.

Second, there is no doubt that both Grant and Ginsberg had deep commitments to a moral and mystical religious vision, but Grant, unlike Ginsberg, would have argued that it is important to hold together spirituality and religion rather than fragmenting them. There is a tendency in Ginsberg to fly off into the mystical, visionary and contemplative ether, and, in the process, such things as dogma and institutions are seen as the problem. Needless to say, such a position becomes its own dogma and institution. Ginsberg's models and teachers were those like Whitman and Blake, whereas for Grant thinkers such as Plato, Augustine, Hooker, Swift, Johnson and Coleridge were his teachers and guides. We can see, therefore, the anti-institutional mindset in Ginsberg, whereas, for Grant, institutions are important even though a critical attitude must always be held towards them. The ideas that underwrite this difference are important to note. Ginsberg's sense of liberty and individualism dominates the day (all so American) whereas for Grant order and institutions are equally important.

Third, although both Ginsberg and Grant howled and lamented the state of things in the 1950s and 1960s, Grant attempted through the Progressive Conservative party, to challenge the American empire. Ginsberg never rose much beyond anarchism, protest politics and moral outrage. Grant pointed out, in *Lament*, how such an approach is both allowed and easily co-opted by the power elites. Those who step out of the formal political process merely facilitate, by their absence, the very thing they protest against. What might seem the moral high ground can be, in fact, a form of grave digging.

Fourth, Grant argued that, with the coming to be of liberalism, we faced an ominous challenge. Those like Daniel Bell had agued (and Grant noticed this) that we had come to the end of ideology with liberalism. Francis Fukuyama argued, in the 1990s, updating Bell's argument, we had come to the end of history with the end of the Cold War and the victory of liberalism. There is no doubt that both Ginsberg and Grant opposed the unilateralism of American military and corporate power. The aggressive notion of liberty and rugged individualism that underwrote and justified such a stance was abhorrent to both Grant and Ginsberg. But—and this is the catch—Ginsberg used the same American notions of liberty and individualism in his anarchist and protest approach as did the power elites. He applied such principles in more of an anti-establishment and, of course, anti-authoritarian way, but the notions of liberty, choice, individualism, protest, dissent were all there.

Grant saw through this charade. Ginsberg was just the other side of the corporate elite. They just used their liberty and freedom in different ways, but neither disagreed about the priority of the American vision and dream: life, liberty, choice and individualism. Grant dared to question the very philosophic principles of American liberalism, and as such, hiked a different path than Ginsberg and the Beats. Canadian notions such as law, order and good government take the curious and thoughtful to different places than life, liberty and the pursuit of happiness. Grant realized that when Canadians uncritically genuflected to the American Beats, they were welcoming the American Trojan horse into Canada in a more subtle way. There are more ways to be colonized than mere military and economic pressures. The literary and cultural traditions of the USA (the Beats) have done much to colonize many Canadians, and there have been many Canadian cultural and literary compradors that have facilitated such a process. Grant would have said No to Ginsberg for the simple reason that Ginsberg was as much a devout and committed American, like a Noam Chomsky, as the very Americans he howled against and opposed.

Fifth, Grant was a much more sophisticated thinker than Ginsberg, and there is no doubt that *Lament for a Nation* is a more substantive work than *Howl*. The level of political and philosophical depth in *Lament* opens up vistas of thought that are just not there in Ginsberg and *Howl*. *Howl* never rises much beyond rant and reaction, and sadly so, Ginsberg's intellectual world tends to polarize between the evil and nasty power elite and the good, pure and lovable anarchist, Beat and protest types. It is a simplistic interpretation of reality that Grant was much too wise to bow an uncritical head to. He saw too much, and saw too far to worship at such a shrine and to such reactionary priests, and he urged Canadians not to turn to such a comic book view of the world.

In sum, Ginsberg and Grant, at first glance, seem to have much in common, but on deeper and further inspection, have little in common. Both protest against many of the same things. Both agree on many of the things that must be opposed. But by day's end, the American Beat anarchism of Ginsberg is quite different from the Canadian High Tory vision of George Grant. It is by understanding such differences that we can see why and how the American and Canadian traditions create and make for different national outlooks. It is somewhat sad and tragic when Canadians know more about American models and take their leads from such fashions than they do from their own kith and kind.

SHEILA GRANT AND LAMENT FOR A NATION

> George Grant always claimed that *Lament for a Nation* had been misunderstood. – Sheila Grant, "Afterword", *Lament for a Nation*

Lament for a Nation has been called "a masterpiece of political meditation" (Peter Emberley) and it "encapsulated the difference between the Tory vision for Canada and the continentalist, mechanistic, commercialist view" (Hugh Segal). There can be no doubt that this compact political missive summed up much about Canadian politics, political theory, philosophy and theology—it has, sadly so, been misread by ideologues that shrink Grant's grander vision of thought and action to their tribal agendas.

Sheila Grant, after George had died (and significantly encouraged by William Christian—one of the finest Grant scholars), wrote an "Afterword" to *Lament for a Nation*—the "Afterword" is a must read for those keen and committed to a fuller understanding of the meaning and significance of *Lament for a Nation*. I was fortunate to meet with Sheila Grant a few times (both at the Grant home on Walnut Street in Halifax and when she visited her daughters in Vancouver on the West Coast of Canada) and we, also, had a lengthy correspondence when she was alive (plus some fine phone conversations)—we talked much about her journey with her husband, George Grant, and the multiple misunderstandings of *Lament*—Sheila's "Afterword" succinctly articulated many of her legitimate concerns.

Sheila began her "Afterword" by suggesting that when the "New Left", in the 1960s, adopted *Lament* as their manifesto of sorts, for a revived form of Canadian nationalism, they misunderstood the more complex nature of the text. Sheila questioned the obstinate fact that many who read *Lament* simply ignored Grant's more ponderous philosophic-theological insights in Chapter VII (that dealt with the tensions between "necessity" and the "good"). Hegel, for Grant, was the dominant philosopher that had done much to be the apologist for the liberal read of history—many follow Hegel in arguing that liberalism is the "necessary" intellectual way of thinking and being for our age and ethos. But, Grant asked, is Hegelian liberalism necessarily "good"? There is an obvious tension between these two ways of living in time and history. Should the thoughtful merely doff their caps and genuflect to the necessity of Hegelian liberalism or is there more to thinking and being than merely an uncritical Yes to Hegel and clan?

There can be no doubt that Chapter VII in *Lament* moves the discussion beyond historic events into the larger realm of liberal necessity (Fukuyama's "end of history") and alternate views of reality worth being open to and living for. Was Grant a determinist and fatalist that assumed there was truly no substantive way to question or oppose the dynamo of Hegelian liberalism? Some have argued such is the case. Sheila Grant, in her "Afterword", makes it abundantly clear that Grant was not a pessimist, cynic or skeptic—"it always matters what each of us does" he often said and "repeated throughout his life". It would be simply foolish to assume Hegelian liberalism would have the ultimate or penultimate word. Sheila made this clear when she stated, "For one who believes, as Grant did, that the spiritual life is open to all, pessimism, is not an option".

Sheila brought to an end her "Afterword", reflecting yet further on George's use of Virgil in Chapter VII, in which those in the direst part of the underworld "beg Charon to rescue them" —their hands reach out to the furthest shore. Was Grant suggesting that, in our time, we were immersed and enfolded in a "sinister region" and did not know it? Was the reaching out of the hands to that further shore a turning against time, history and matter to a better world, a world beyond the Platonic world of shadows? Or, as Sheila suggests, was George Grant looking for and gazing at the "good" that could orient those in time to a sounder and more meaningful manner?

The final couple of paragraphs in the "Afterword" bring the reader to one of Grant's favourite places—Terence Bay, where coast, rock, weather and water mix and intermingle. I have had the privilege of spending time at the Grant cabin at

Terence Bay and sat on the time worn rocks that overlook both the bay and ocean. Sheila rightly suggested that it was the "austere and unchanging beauty" of Terence Bay that became for Grant "an image of the timeless: a holy place. From a cabin he built on a hill, he would look across the ocean inlet to the towering rocks on the further shore, and quote the line that ends *Lament for a Nation*".

Chapter VII in *Lament*, as Sheila rightly suggests, is central to Grant's political, philosophical and theological jeremiad and masterpiece—those who ignore Chapter VII will misread the deeper purpose of *Lament* and distort Grant's larger questions and concerns. There is, in short, much more to *Lament* than merely a lament, and the journey into Grant's distinction between Hegelian "necessity" and the Platonic "good" is the entrée portal—Sheila Grant, in the "Afterword", pointed the way—Chapter VII is now the meditative challenge before us.